Also by Aaron Kent

SELECTED POETRY:

Tertiary Colours (Knives, Forks, and Spoons, 2018)

The Last Hundred (Guillemot Press, 2019)

Melatonin Spring Collection (Invisible Hand, 2020)

Harbour Equinox (Alban Low, 2020)

Angels the Size of Houses (Shearsman, 2021)

Collected Pamphlets (Broken Sleep Books, 2021)

PROSE:

My Glorious Sundays (Broken Sleep Books, 2021)

EDITOR (SELECTED):

Crossing Lines (Broken Sleep Books, 2021)

Snackbox (Broken Sleep Books, 2021)

THE RISE OF

———————————

Aaron Kent

ISBN: 978-1-915079-81-7

The author has asserted their right to be identified as the author of this Work in accordance with the Copyright, Designs and Patents Act 1988

Cover designed by Aaron Kent

Edited and typeset by Aaron Kent

Broken Sleep Books Ltd
Rhydwen,
Talgarreg,
SA44 4HB
Wales

Contents

I started reading it…I couldn't stop. Incredibly impactful, heartbreaking, terrifying, raw but deeply authentic. *The Rise Of...* doesn't allow you to take a breath. It holds you in its grip and drills every single word into your skull. In trying to break away from his past, Kent gets dragged backwards again and again into a polaroid box full of haunted visions and feelings. The actual survival of trauma is very much like this. Important to acknowledge, not just for Kent, but for survivors in general. Men need to be able to express their grief of trauma and sexual assault. It needs opening up and this does it.

— Stuart McPherson, *Waterbearer*

We're dropped, with immediacy and intimacy, into a body of work which fills every available space on the page in order to explore its subject: an incidence of sexual abuse and the fallout that follows.

This is not a stream of consciousness it's a flood.

The text feels as if it's being written as we read it. We follow Aaron between moments of matter-of-fact lucidity, landing blows with uncomplicated language: "I had surgery to fix the damage on my throat and I lost the ability to vomit," and surrealist poignancy, where the poets urge to make beautiful slips through: "The broken boats bubbles spilling onto the plates as I swallow down the shark that ran me on its metal teeth".

This piece of writing exhausted me, as any revolutionary writing should. Punctuation is abandoned to demonstrate the structural damage sexual abuse can do to its victims, leaving those of us who read it start to finish literally breathless. But it's last page makes a break for air, through deep water, and manages a defiant hope, proof of survival to all of us who need it.

— Day Mattar, *Springing from the Pews*

The Rise Of...

Aaron Kent

I don't write letters much anymore but i used to In the months that followed the sexual assault i had written or rewritten at least fifty letters which i would pretend to send to men i thought were least likely to understand In my letters i tried to convey the things that happened to me hoping to find ways i could make sense of it The first letter i wrote was kind of an apology even though i was still trying to justify what happened still trying to find a good reason for why i had come home you know When i saw the doctor i cried a little When i lied and used my parasomnia to get discharged i cried less After i continued writing trying to craft the most elaborate letters each trying to convince someone that i wasn't insane and i was just a coward who didn't have the courage to report it After a few months i grew frustrated and stopped trying to justify what happened and stopped writing The thing was that i had learned how to survive life in a shell and i had learned to live without sleep I didn't eat well and i stopped playing basketball and started drinking heavily and eventually my partner convinced me to attempt therapy but that was years after and the therapists didn't help at first The first summer i tried to fuck as many people as I could but i was too drunk most of the time and i had no time to write not even letters as i tended to do on the weekends Hallucinations disturbed me nightly of a being that looked like my attacker's father's father and of an abstract shape that moved almost levitated against a wall Waking up from these felt like living as i went straight to wanting to convince myself that what happened hadn't happened I found that i could often pretend that it hadn't happened if i just kept watching too much TV Or read a book I was sick of life so sick of even attempting sleep so tired of screaming and the low moans of the neighbours watching soap operas so clearly i could almost swear they were speaking to me In a strange and desperate attempt to console myself i began writing love letters to men i didn't particularly like Through these i thought if i write enough love letters then someday someone will read them and they will love me and take me away from the noise and the lights and the nightmares and away from the dirt under my nails and i will be free It was wrong i was wrong but it felt so good to write the letters that i could not stop I was sixteen when i first found a man i wanted to fuck I told him to come over and i took a shower When i stepped out of the shower i was completely nude the door was locked and the bed was covered with a comforter so heavy and soft that i could barely move the thing When i reached to grab the blankets my arm was entangled in a large ugly long purple tree frog He had nestled in between my left arm and my right leg which were locked in a sort of claw The frog was fully capable of sinking its spikes into my right leg and i was completely petrified I fell onto the bed trying to get away from the tree frog but i tripped and fell onto the comforter and the tree frog began biting at my arms and legs trying to eat me The more i fought against it the more i became weak and defeated until i had managed to get some of the large bites to form a bloody puss on my right arm The frog was trying to eat me i could not lose I crawled to the door and i threw the door open yelling at the man telling him that i had been bitten by a monster He looked down at me with that odd patient look and said It's not a monster darling And it wasn't but i refused to believe him I refused to believe that the thing that had entered my flat in my bedroom was not a monster In my mind i could see the dirt under my fingernails could see the scars on my inner thigh could see the deep cuts across my chest and i believed that they could belong to something ugly and unnatural As it began to gain momentum i could feel its body become stronger harder more aggressive I tried to hold onto my rational thought but i was losing and the monster was stronger I looked older and i looked older and older I was not a child When i was not a teenager i had been with 4 people in my life 2 men and 2 women but i guess if you include a lack of consent i had been with 5 people in my life 3 men and 2 women I had hallucinations again of a being that looked nothing like him and of an abstract shape that moved almost levitated against a wall In the last years the only time i've written letters has been when I was particularly manic After my diagnosis with Borderline Personality Disorder i wondered if he pushed the illness into me Was BPD sexually transmitted I wanted to write letters about rape I wanted to write letters about mental illness I wanted to write letters about how toxic masculinity is killing us all I wanted to write about killing him again and again and again until i was burned out on the pain and confusion and pain and misery and pain and fury that my youth had left me with and i had no words left I would try to make these letters beautiful to illustrate a sunny side of the darkness that was overwhelming me I thought if i could do that i might gain some small relief from it at least in my mind The difficulty with this approach is that really i was trying to convince myself that i was okay It was an obsessive attempt to reconcile the two sides of myself and a shame-based attempt at recovery Of course there was no simple resolution to my mental illness or my assault but there was something i desperately wanted to believe I wanted to say i had won but i gave up calling myself a survivor or a victim I gave up calling myself on the phone That was a struggle a hard battle an intellectual fight with and between myself and an idea that had taken over my mind and no longer allowed for an honest representation of my trauma Years had passed and my pain had moved I felt like a shadow of my former self diminished in size in consciousness and in my world The monster had started to slowly reassert itself and i would try and force my mouth to say i was okay but it refused to let me It demanded i accept that i was broken that i was not the same guy who had listened to shrimp give a round of applause for a career It demanded that i be a stranger to myself And when i had been on that path for so long the monster had ceased needing a place to rest I gave up on myself I could not hold myself together I felt my body shutting down I went into what i call my minimal autonomy mode where i would be awake and alert and aware but i would almost completely disengage from the world I would have thought that this was why i was still alive But the truth was that i was alive because i did not care enough to kill myself I did not care about myself or my life or the people i loved or my family I did not care what people thought I did not care what people said I could see nothing hear nothing and see no one I would walk around and i would have the sensation that my entire body was turning into a void But if you blinked you would miss me I did not care about myself I did not care about my family or my friends or my students or my cats And i was profoundly lonely horribly lonely My parents would tell me that they cared and my brothers would tell me that they cared but it was a joke that you tell because it makes you feel better I could hear them and see them and their words seemed to do nothing to stop the sunless reality that filled my head I did not know how to care I did not know how to connect

I was empty and alone I did not know how to make myself feel better In my mind the assault that i had suffered was now my identity it was who i was I felt worthless broken used My physical self did not matter and i did not care about my body I could not feel safe anywhere but i felt particularly unsafe in the space between my flat and my car I would run a short distance from my flat from the front of the flat and to the car door If i heard a car coming i would run back to my flat As the car drove away i would stare at the spot where it had been I wanted to feel safe but i didn't know how When i drove home i always drove home with my windows down music on full blast even in torrential rain or hail I would stop driving and pull into dead ends and i would just sit in the car inside a car while it was raining outside rocking back and forth I did not have friends or family who understood this they never had because i had not let them I didn't want anyone to understand I didn't want anyone to care about me I didn't want anyone to give a shit If i could tell my attacker about what happened afterward about this aftermath would that make it better Would he think twice Would i be fixed Would i not be a piece of shit Would i be able to move on to heal Revenge would make me feel better revenge would make me feel complete I would wait When i was at my lowest point i was raptured in my seldom sleep as i wondered if my soul was going to slip out my mouth when i swallowed my final breath I imagined telling him all about it hoping that it would bring me comfort like he might have been able to feel me and care and i wouldn't be alone anymore I guess the rapture was too early cause i fell right back down my body like a door being slammed in the face crashed to the ground The night terrors always felt hypnagogic but after an hour i knew i was real and i knew what he did was real and in my pain i really did feel like i was alone even when i was lying in bed with strangers I was alone I was lonely It was incredibly hard at group therapy to broach and deal with what had happened to me I didn't really know how to process it I felt angry and sad I felt confused and lost and scared I felt like i couldn't trust people and i didn't know why I spent the first few weeks really the first few months just trying to navigate the whole survivor thing It's a confusing game to be a survivor There should be someone around you who's your best guess of having done it first and there is There was a whole therapy session of biscuits and coffee but instead it felt like having been assaulted by everyone I was the victim of a man who had been spent for a few years and had had a couple kids I had surgery to fix the damage on my throat and i lost the ability to vomit but my body began to heal faster Now i had a complex about that I dreamt of being raptured again but before my body had time to absorb the experience a whole bunch of others disappeared for good passing by my window I was angry I felt

like i had been ripped off No compensation
No thanks Just an inability to pass anything
back up my throat I wondered if his
destruction of me had made me unviable as
a rapturable option Some time passed and i
got a job i liked it It was more than just a job
it was something I was a stronger guy than
i had been I had also been thinking of
leaving group therapy I thought about
what i had gone through in my life and i
wondered if it was possible to do anything
i wanted if I put my mind to it If i ever
made a move to get back to normal i wanted
to be able to get it right I tried to do the
things other people had been doing I went
to the shops and bought stuff and generally
looked the part of someone who is not
missing Well that was until i had a rapture

night terror again i went home and lay in bed for three weeks There was no more rapture to be had I had a new lease of life I felt a lot better My body was no longer riddled with infection I had a new body and this new lease of life And so my new job as a rapturable person began I started opening up to the people that had come back before me The previous rapturers They had also been given their new lease of life They were happy and that made me happy Their therapy check ins were full of adventure and progression and some even felt strong enough to actually leave I thought it might never have been possible to do that I wanted to do that but i'd have nowhere left to cry on a weekly basis My last session was in August of 2017 That was a tough session Saying goodbye to people i had broken down in front of for years I went home and cried in the garden and a year after i met a man who had been to the same sessions and his grandson had died and his son had been hit by lightning twice but he was ok He had found another group and they had saved him He told me he had been pulled up and sucked into a box of light but he had survived it I'm like a sponge i'm always shedding and if i don't deal with it the pain won't go away I think of all the things that make me feel like crying or screaming My skin My eyes Sometimes the silence can be too loud Sometimes i feel like i'm hearing too much like the world has started spitting at me the way it would spit at the kid with the blistered and bleeding skin who wasn't wearing shoes to school That kid was me I know it's unreasonable to be bothered by things like that but i can't stop myself it's almost like a phobia i think A fear I think about people i know who keep themselves together I don't understand it do they know how to display emotion Do they even care about holding themselves together like leaning on a balcony railing pulling the universe into one And what about the day i stopped being surprised by the sound of my own crying It will always be there in the background letting me know there are other things going on in the world and that i should just get over myself already My hand is itching My leg is itching Sometimes it's all i can do to focus on the horizon because the itching is so bad i have to remember to breathe because the itching is telling me to scratch my skin until it bleeds so deeply he leaves Sometimes i just bite down until the itching stops I guess that's what people mean when they say i don't know myself I think i'll try to make some music for which i don't know the words but i know the feeling There must be a word for losing melody At this point in my life i would rather just scream There's something so simple and powerful about that Mostly i will leave my skin alone because it is mine Mine to deal with I will choose to focus on all the good things all the things i can see rather than those things that are hidden I'm starting to realize that some of those things i can't see maybe they should be seen Perhaps it's better to acknowledge the pain instead of running from it If i don't accept it i will never get better The thing i want most in the world is to be able to walk outside and feel my feet touch the ground To just stand there for a while looking at the sky when i can see the stars a little bit I hope that when i am done with the moon there will be a bridge where i can get over to the other side and touch the stars and sit down My friends thought i had invented it Actually in fact everyone thought i had made it all up I dreamt for the first time in my life of losing all my teeth They fell out like therapy members from my life and it felt like the dream logic was obvious and it was but i had found movement and progression and love and family even when my body started to feel the darkness crawl over me The darkness had so long been waiting to get me before it could grab hold of me and i struggled to stay alert My body ached from fatigue I lost control i lost control i was completely powerless My body broke down The broken pieces started to feel whole The broken pieces of me started to become stronger than the broken pieces of him *You can feel it You can feel it Please don't close your eyes anymore please don't close your eyes Please don't close your eyes anymore Please don't close your eyes Please don't close your eyes anymore Please don't close your eyes anymore* I kept on fighting i kept on fighting to live I had to keep on living i couldn't let it end i couldn't let it end *I'm here for you now I'm here for you now I'm here for you now I'm here for you now I'm here for you now I'm here for you now It's a night terror wake up baby Please don't close your eyes anymore Please don't close your eyes again Please don't close your eyes again You are here and i'm here No one should have to go through this no one should have to be scared to face that monster When it's gonna come i can be brave You can be brave too Fighting your struggle to hide* He haunts me *But now I'm fighting for you* No let it come and i'll heal Sometimes life gives you a huge fucking lemon rips into you good and throws you into the sewer and rain pours on you over and over and round and round We all die Sometimes i may even share my deepest darkest scars I know i can beat the man but i've been broken i've grown and came back together and i'm not sure i can do that again Devastated individuals often receive their abusive experience as an impression of who they are and some become the worst versions of themselves I didn't feel like i had much of a past before being sexually battered anyway The depersonalisation was already strong from the age of 12 so i was in the clouds as i watched myself get assaulted In the first draft of this book i still couldn't bring myself to talk about being sexually violated so i used a weird heavy metaphor That's not what i want to talk about I want to talk about how great i feel And sometimes i am happy i am but i can't be the guy who is too broken for joy I don't want to talk about how I've been ripped apart or glued back together with tape and dental floss The night-terrors were never about him but they were always about him I remember looking in the mirror as my skin peeled off It didn't make sense that this new healing process would take months of intense repetitive reaping and sheathing away parts like a ritual of something the nervous system couldn't help anyway Why wouldn't i rip off my skin so i could grow out new skin to take up the slack I couldn't talk about the night terrors the day after How my body ached and sometimes my limbs still froze up for no reason I dreamt that afterwards he was apologetic but he never was in reality A day later he begged for me to visit him during the off-shift and told me i had ruined his life and changed him forever and he couldn't live without me He asked me to give him oral sex while the rest watched I heard him tell somebody that it was a gift to get caught by a miracle He called himself a miracle I closed my eyes so he couldn't see me but i was still being snatched by his fingers and he could tell as i felt my skin going back over my bones Nobody wanted to save me after i had been rammed into the harbour floor by him when they released us from the vessel But this isn't an open letter to him I didn't ask for an apology but people told me i should I didn't see the point I am always on that submarine begging to be raptured I can still feel it now from my body back into the sea into the ocean into his bed The broken boats bubbles spilling onto the plates as i swallow down the shark that ran me on its metal teeth There is a part of me that can still hear this with cavitation at 4 kilohertz Like taking blows from his body's mechanical semen There is always someone who will put me in a submarine It used to be anyone a random man who i met at a bar or someone i had met in another city or a waitress who didn't remember me when they saw me at the restaurant a week later But i got better and found the only person putting me back was me I had found myself in the shadows of every movie i had found myself on every television show and i told myself i looked like i was once great I'm always with me I found a whole bunch of things to live for and i lived and i nearly died and i lived again and i assumed this history would fade into obsoletion but it sticks around in the textbooks and that's why it shook me that there were still photos in the book Even when i'm happy and away there are still photos and i guess i was not prepared to return to this I thought the scab would heal and depart but it never does it just scars and sometimes in the heat the scar swells and i've got to learn to be ok with that It doesn't mean I'm there again It doesn't mean I'm broken It just means i carry my reminders It means i'm the one who runs the boat and i'm the one who has to dive back in and be taken There's a boat in the ocean You can't have the ocean unless there is a boat I am going to leave the boat and there will be a boat My name is on the boat The ocean will get bigger and bigger I can't stop it and you can't stop it It's a one way thing I can't get out and i can't get in I am always on the boat and i can't hear the ocean but i take my boat out to the place where the boat is a boat and no one is the boat He is not the boat I am not the boat I am the ocean The ocean is me I can have the ocean and the boat and i can kick him off the boat I am the boat and the ocean I am everything i want to hold on to.

I am the boat!

I am the ocean!

I am the rapture!

Inkmist

For CRASAC group therapy; for saving me

The last night
we played like
children gathering feathered
flags, each of us
carrying birds exposed
in our violent mouths.
The universe's silence
began to enact itself as
a rainbow's communion.
Then our bird-mouths
deepened, fragmented,
a hundred words overlapped.
Flowers rose around a
walnut veneer door,
and we were bird noise
instead of voices.

Us, lifted into a light,
the light and the light
in its first day; my blindness
astray in its own volley,
extinguishing the sun.
Lightly on my shoulder
the world came to write
obituaries on the beaks of birds.

Acknowledgements

Thank you, in no particular order, to these people who saved me:

Emma
CRASAC (Steve Joy Gavin and Jake)
Rue
Otis
Jenő
Stuart
Mum and Dad
Andy Mac
Azad
Day
Joe Luke and Adam
Dean
Pancho
Jenni
Fran and Liz
Kate
Matteo
Charlie
UHW

LAY OUT YOUR RAPTURE

Lightning Source UK Ltd.
Milton Keynes UK
UKHW051341060322
399623UK00006B/217